Co-consciousness

Debbie Pearl

Table of contents:

Chapter 1: What is Co-consciousness?

The experience of someone with plurality, when more than one portion is aware of what is happening, is referred to as co-consciousness. When a separate component of a person with DID (formerly known as multiple personality disorder) is absent, they often become amnesic because of their very high degrees of dissociation in identity and memory. Amnesia may result in upsetting events like forgetting crucial personal details like your name, date of birth, or home address, years of your life, or everyday challenges like "waking up" in a strange location without knowing how you got there. Some individuals are acutely aware of how quickly time passes or how quickly memories fade, while others are in a sort of confusing fog up until someone inquires, "Where did you buy those shoes?" How recently did you last eat? What did you do on Wednesday? they aren't even aware that they are suffering from forgetfulness.

With typical DID, the person not only has amnesia but is also perplexed by evidence that has been left behind while other pieces have been removed. The obvious items may include family members furious over disagreements you don't remember having, friends who believe they know you by a different name, clothing in the closet that are foreign and not to their liking, etc.

Co-consciousness refers to switching without this amnesia, such that if one half is out living their life, another part is aware of what is going on. High co-consciousness multiples don't often "lose time" or slip into a coma; instead, they remain mindful of what is happening. Although my levels of forgetfulness rise under stress, this is primarily how I operate. For many multiples, regaining some level of co-consciousness is a crucial component of treatment and recovery work. Multiples with high degrees of amnesia often feel that this is one of the most difficult and terrifying elements of their illness. The first steps in this approach often include developing self awareness and system mapping.

Practically, co-consciousness may function in a few distinct ways. Even though they are not the ones manipulating the body, some multiples experience it as if they are seeing and hearing all that is happening. Others may want to hear about what occurred or see a little film of recollections. When I was younger, I used to find it strange that so many of my own memories are in the third person rather than the first person, meaning that I always seem to be looking down on everyone, including myself. Since then, I've learned that this is a simple method for me to determine when I've been actively moving my body and when I've simply been co-consciously observing. Co-conscious recollections are told in the third person, whereas my personal memories are told in the first. Everyone experiences this differently, however! In unfamiliar situations or with new acquaintances, I may sometimes really struggle, particularly if I haven't met them or been there before. When I ask for information internally, others may notice when I hesitate, and if I'm fortunate, the portion that recognizes the person or recalls the incident may swiftly fill me in, or swap out and take over.

Co-consciousness has many benefits but also drawbacks. For me, one of them is the enormous energy required to keep track of all the many pieces of information and memories and pass them back and forth. On a busy day, it seems like I have file cabinets in every area of my home, and I'm mentally bouncing back and forth between them to make sure we can keep up and still work as a team. Multiples who have only been exposed to the concepts of psychosis or DID and don't believe they match either category may be perplexed by the sensation of co-consciousness. Being conscious of what is happening but lacking self-control can also be upsetting. I remember being horrified by a lot of childhood encounters to the point that I thought I was being possessed by the devil. When I looked in the mirror, I would be scared to see this face that was my but nonetheless unmistakably wasn't me. I frequently felt at battle with myself, fighting to remain out and in control. When you're co-conscious, you could simultaneously feel surrounded and agonizingly alone. Schneiderian first-rank symptoms are what are known as these experiences, and they were originally considered to be quite diagnostic of schizophrenia. We are now learning that dissociative individuals really experience these things rather often.

Aside from the technical details, how does co-consciousness feel? Well, it depends on the individual. In fact, various portions of my body have their own unique experiences with it. The person in the field is often aware of whether they are handling things alone or whether other portions are "near to the surface" and aware of what is happening. When those surfacing sections are trying to switch or are being prompted to switch, they may sometimes remark or provide advice about what they are seeing. For instance, I recently delivered a discussion in a closed ward of a mental hospital, and it was going well. There was a sizable crowd waiting when we arrived with the notes and presentation equipment, and we had the appropriate person there who had previously prepared and presented the lecture. There was a little hiccup since the radio was playing a depressing, lonely tune. A melancholy, lonely side of me was quickly drawn to the surface by the music, which may be a strong trigger for me. As they were aware that they couldn't make the presentation and really want to be somewhere, we began to get a little anxious. Finally, the MC switched down the radio to introduce us while we remained still and silent. When the music stopped, that portion went back inside and the proper portion emerged to give the speech. Phew! Being a multiple may be quite difficult.

Chapter 2: History of Consciousness.

For thousands of years, philosophers have devoted the majority of their labor to the study of human consciousness. The theory of mind-body dualism, or the notion that while the mind and body are distinct, they do interact, was first put out by the French philosopher Rene Descartes.

As soon as psychology was recognized as a field distinct from philosophy and biology, early psychologists began focusing on the study of conscious experience.

Introspection was a technique employed by structuralists to examine and record conscious feelings, ideas, and experiences. The contents of their own brains would be thoroughly examined by trained observers. Although this was undoubtedly a highly personal experience, it served as inspiration for more investigation into the field of consciousness research.

In spite of ongoing shifts and changes, consciousness remains unbroken and continuous, according to American psychologist William James. Sigmund Freud, a psychoanalyst, concentrated on comprehending the significance of the unconscious and conscious minds.

The study of human consciousness has advanced significantly since the 1950s, despite the fact that most of psychology research throughout the first half of the 20th century turned its emphasis to merely observable actions.

The absence of a widely acknowledged operational definition of consciousness is one of the issues in studying it. Cogito ergo sum, or "I think, therefore I am," is a concept put forward by Descartes. It holds that the act of thinking itself proves that one is aware and exists. Even though an awareness of oneself and the outside environment is the most common definition of consciousness today, there are still disagreements over the many components of this awareness.

Understanding the neurobiology behind our conscious experiences has been the focus of research on consciousness. Researchers have even used brain-scanning equipment to look for certain neurons that may be connected to various conscious occurrences. The integrated information theory and the global workspace theory are the two main theories of consciousness put forward by contemporary scholars.

Chapter 3: Time loss, Black outs.

A time period for which one or more alters cannot account because another alter was present in the body or mind at that time. Dissociative identity disorder (DID) and a few instances of other defined dissociative disorder, subtype 1 are the only parts-based dissociative disorders that exhibit this distinct kind of dissociative amnesia (OSSD-1). The amount of time lost may range from a few seconds to many years. When Alter B becomes active again at age 10, for instance, if Alter A is the host from years 7-9 and Alter B is not present at all during this time, Alter B may not remember anything that happened during this time. Alter B, on the other hand, may be able to access Alter A's or another alter's memories after they have awoke in order to get some insight into what happened while they were asleep. Alter B could have received brief flashes of knowledge about the outside world at this time, even though they were dormant from years 7-9. Dissociative boundaries between alters are not real, concrete objects, and information may pass across them more often than one would think.

When an alter blacks out, there is a certain kind of temporal loss that takes place. When one or more alters are unconscious while one or more other alters utilize the body, this is known as a black out. Many alters may suffer a full episode of time loss in which they do not exist, while other alters may just feel as if time is flowing slowly or as though they are stuck in darkness. Blackouts may cause time loss that many people find unsettling. Black outs are often seen as overwhelming proof of either DID or some other neurological issue that is likely not trauma-related. Black outs may seem confrontational and may cause denial episodes when the person or alter refuses to believe they have DID, were abused, or are anything but a liar, phony, or "crazy."

Alters who have blacked out, on the other hand, may not be aware that they have lost time and could feel hostile or upset if they are shown signs of memory gaps. Amnesia may mask amnesia, making a person believe they have no sense of time passing until it is shown otherwise. The presence of objects, works of art, or writings that the individual does not recognize but that could not have been purchased or produced by other household members, the use of an unfamiliar name by strangers who behave familiarly around the individual, or being questioned about alleged actions that the individual cannot recall or does not believe they would ever commit are all signs of time loss. An altar would sometimes go through a dissociative fugue and then find themselves in a new place with no memory of how they got there. This might be as simple as "waking up" in another room or as serious as discovering they have unknowingly moved to a different state. The person might abruptly "wake up" in the midst of or at the conclusion of a discussion or activity. They may not be able to remember some parts of their past. They could suddenly find that they cannot recall anything from before they moved out of their home at the age of 18, or their whole childhood may be blank.

Even while all blacked-out alters are losing time, not all blacked-out alters are also losing time. While an alter may temporarily lose awareness of the outer world, they may still be somewhat active and conscious inside their own minds. An alter may spend what seems like a week inside before returning to the outer world to discover that months have passed while they were gone since internal worlds may not always exist in tandem with the outside world. In this scenario, the alter doesn't feel as if they were totally unconscious of everything, but rather as though they were unaware of the outside world and its events.

Not all switches cause time to pass faster. Co-consciousness, or the capacity for two or more alters to be simultaneously present in the body or aware of the outside world, has been developed in many systems to varying degrees. Co-conscious alters, sometimes known as co-cons, may or may not have various levels of control over their bodies and may or may not be aware of one another's thoughts and emotions. Different systems are built with different levels of co-consciousness. Others may discover that they may become co-conscious so quickly that it is difficult to resist falling into denial that they ever lose any time at all. Some people may need to labor for years to develop a workable state of co-consciousness between a few highly communicative alters. When people get complacent and cease looking out for memory gaps or other indications of unremembered events, typically high levels of co-consciousness may actually serve to disguise black out switches.

Co-consciousness does not always extend to all alters, even within a same system. It's possible that only Alter A can be co-aware of Alter C, but Alters A and B may always be cognizant of one another. Alter E may not be aware of any of the other alters, and Alter D might be able to observe the other alters even if they are unaware of the other alters and their behaviors in return, and Alter E might not be aware of any of the other alters either! Alter H may only sometimes or under certain circumstances be co-conscious with Alter A, while Alters F and G may be co-conscious with each other but must leave post-it notes for the rest of the system to communicate. Later I had the choice to accept or deny others' co-consciousness.

Co-fronting is a special kind of co-consciousness. Co-fronting refers to when two or more alters are simultaneously controlling the body to differing degrees. Alters may, to varied degrees, be aware of each other's acts or claim them as their own.

The person may feel "partial intrusions" without knowing or comprehending where these arise when two or more alters are mutually present but one alter is not completely aware of this. One may have ideas or feelings that seem external to themselves or that "came out of nowhere," as such as hearing internal voices, discussions, or tears. One may also be astonished by acts or statements that they did not plan to do or were about to take. In certain circumstances, the person may also suffer a brief identity change or confusion, such as a sudden unsureness about their true nature, interests, and ideas, as well as their sexual orientation or gender. These experiences might be misconstrued for psychosis by the patient or an inexperienced physician, however the cause of these symptoms is dissociative in nature. These sensations may be seen as less terrifying or startling after the person is more aware of their separate components (because their origin is recognized), or as more frightening once they are (because they can no longer be rationalized away).

No one of the participating components is guaranteed complete memory access just because they are co-conscious or co-fronting. When a part is present that is not supposed to know this information is present, alters may occasionally find that information is blocked from them. For instance, specific trauma details may not be retrievable if bringing them to memory could make them known to a host that could not tolerate them. Similarly, when a part is no longer in communication with another part, information may sometimes be lost to that part; for example, if Alters A and B are both present for a distressing occurrence, certain elements of that event may only be known to Alter B after it has concluded. Furthermore, if an alter lacks knowledge or abilities, their presence can make it difficult or impossible for other alters to remember this information.

Due to influence from a much younger portion, this might manifest as someone suddenly forgetting their address, how to do a simple job activity, or who their spouse is. On the other hand, people could discover that they unexpectedly acquire knowledge that they would have swore they did not have, such as the ability to speak in a language they haven't spoken since they were young. Finally, certain alters may purposefully obstruct access to memories or even information from other portions. If people attempt to access this knowledge, they can discover that their minds abruptly become blank or that they are suddenly driven into a new mental route.

It should be emphasized that not all memory problems are always linked to specific alterations. Sometimes people have memory lapses as a result of alcohol or other drug use, a brain injury, or a neurological condition. Strong dissociation may affect memory recall for certain alters, but it can also affect memory encoding in the forms of derealization or depersonalization. Cognitive diversion, exhaustion, or physical discomfort may potentially prevent memories from being properly encoded. The memories may be said to be kept in a dissociated part (particularly, an emotional part), although this part may just retain the painful memory and not qualify as an alter, leading to dissociative amnesia in reaction to traumatic experiences even in people without DID. In this manner, experiences from childhood or maturity may be forgotten in OSDD-1 patients who do not typically have amnesia.

Chapter 4: Diagnosis.

Dissociative identity disorder is frequently misdiagnosed as schizophrenia or other psychotic illnesses, affective disorders, drug misuse disorders, or personality disorders, and people with it frequently spend many years in the mental health system (most commonly borderline personality disorder). Most notably, the Dissociative Experiences Scale (DES), the Somatoform Dissociation Questionnaire (SDQ-20), and the "gold-standard," the Structured Clinical Interview for DSM-IV Disorders, are three well-validated screening instruments accessible to qualified professionals to aid in diagnosis (SCID-D). Despite this, it's possible that most DID sufferers won't get a proper diagnosis since some mental health specialists don't think the disorder "exists," despite the wealth of research to the contrary.

Working with Altar Personalities:

At some time during therapy, a client with dissociative identity disorder will undoubtedly come with their "alternative personalities," also referred to as "alters," "parts," etc. These might appear to have various ages, genders, traits, and frequently varying degrees of knowledge of their autobiography. Others will not. While there is no co-consciousness, there will frequently be brief amnesic gaps when that part is "out" or "under executive control." Some "parts" of the personality will be aware of or "co-conscious" with other "parts," while others will not. For the client, who may feel as though they are "going mad" because they are unsure of what they did or said in the moments, hours, or (rarely) days prior, this can be upsetting and disturbing.

Remember that the components "are not truly different identities or personalities in one body, but rather components of a single personality that are not yet operating together in a smooth, coordinated, and adaptable fashion." The goal of therapy is to help these components work together more effectively and maybe even "fuse" or raise their level of coordination. Working on improved collaboration and communication between parts frequently results in higher degrees of co-consciousness, which can give DID clients a sense of more control over their lives.

There are several useful methods for comprehending and organizing these many "pieces" in terms of the part they play in the person's life as a whole. The Apparently Normal Personalities (ANPs) and the Emotional Personalities (EPs), who are "stuck" in those experiences and experience them as now rather than as past, are fundamentally different, according to Van der Hart et altheory .'s of "structural dissociation." The former are typically preoccupied with moving on with life and manage by blocking out memories and experiences related to the past traumatic events, while the latter are "stuck" in those experiences and experience them as now rather.

In treating dissociative identity disorder, a large portion of therapy is focused on resolving conflicts between this fundamental split and a deeper level of conflicts between various EPs' preferred "survival reaction," such as fight, flee, freeze, or submit. The causal trauma is the center of the entire personality, which is built around either experiencing it (via the EPs) or avoiding it (the ANPs). Finding effective strategies for dealing with all of the many components of the personality can be made possible with the aid of the structural dissociation theory.

Although there has been much discussion and disagreement over whether or not dealing with "alternative personalities" is therapeutic, the ISSTD guidelines1 do recommend doing so in a non-judgmental, encouraging manner. This allows the therapist to serve as a "relational bridge," allowing the client to connect with and relate to all of the dissociated and disowned aspects of themselves, including as personality traits, repressed emotions, and painful experiences. However, the therapist must keep in mind that the client is a single person with multiple distinct parts and must not encourage unneeded additional development or autonomy of "alters" in order to prevent separation.

Fostering integration between disjointed emotions, memories, behaviors, and sense of identity should be the therapeutic objective. Increased associative functioning should take precedence over total "fusion" of the different personalities into one whole, which may not always be attainable. For some patients, "stable multiplicity" may be a more realistic therapy result.

Working with people who have dissociative identity disorder is challenging and frequently ongoing. For the therapist doing this treatment, there will be a variety of problems and difficulties. But it may also be some of the most fulfilling psychotherapy work, and individuals with dissociative identity disorder can have extremely favorable prognoses as a result of receiving good, efficient therapy.

Chapter 5: Treatment.

Dissociative identity disorder is best treated with long-term, one-on-one, relationally focused psychotherapy. The majority of the time, treatment will take place at least once per week, but this will rely on a variety of variables, including the client's level of functioning, resources, support, and motivation. Therapy may last for five years or longer, and lengthier sessions (of 75 to 90 minutes, or even longer) are frequently necessary. It can also be beneficial to employ a variety of treatments, including sensorimotor psychotherapy, eye movement desensitization and reprocessing (EMDR), dialectical behavior therapy, and cognitive behavioral therapy.

However, EMDR procedures must be modified for use with DID since normal EMDR therapy, particularly when administered by a professional who is not knowledgeable with dissociative disorders, can result in a dangerous flooding of traumatic information and a client's subsequent destabilization.

Phase-oriented therapy is generally agreed to be the most successful. The three steps that are most often employed are:

- Creating a secure environment achieving stability and reducing symptoms.
- Processing and integrating traumatic experiences.
- Integration and rehabilitation.

In practice, it is doubtful that the work will go in a straight line through these three stages; instead, it will often spiral through each one, with numerous stops in the middle and latter stages to return to stabilization work. A third area of therapy is "attachment," with the great majority of clients with dissociative identity disorder arriving with disordered attachment patterns. This area of treatment is in addition to dealing with dissociative symptoms and processing and integrating the underlying trauma.

Many dissociative identity disorder patients experience acute and ongoing trauma, which can result in complicated and variable transference and countertransference reactions throughout therapy. The topic of boundaries must be handled with extreme caution since many people with dissociative identity disorder have a history of boundary breaches, which increases the risk of reenactments in therapy settings. At every level of the treatment, limits must be discussed and agreed upon in an open and honest manner. "Crisis" can happen frequently during treatment, although it's more likely to happen when working with painful memories in phase 2. It's crucial to have flexible boundaries that maintain the therapeutic frame, especially when working with patients who have attachment disorders.

The biggest indicator of therapeutic success is the strength of the relationship between the therapist and the client, therefore finding a therapist who possesses these qualities and is also flexible and prepared to work with clients for an extended period of time on really upsetting material is crucial. It is advisable to seek specialized supervision from a professional with experience treating dissociative disorders and to prevent isolation by joining encouraging professional communities working in this area. Due to the serious and persistent nature of the abuse encountered by the majority of individuals with dissociative identity disorder, consideration must always be given to the potential of secondary traumatization.